DESSERTS

Carole Handslip

HAMLYN

CONTENTS

Soufflés, Mousses & Charlottes 6

Creams, Custards & Puddings 16

Fruit Desserts 32

Frozen Desserts 44

Pies, Tarts & Cheesecakes 58

Cakes & Cookies 66

Special Occasion Desserts 76

This edition published in 1990 by
The Hamlyn Publishing Group Limited,
a division of the Octopus Publishing Group,
Michelin House, 81 Fulham Road,
London SW3 6RB

ISBN 0 600 56999 3

Produced by Mandarin Offset
Printed and Bound in Hong Kong

This edition prepared under the supervision
of Joanna Morris

INTRODUCTION

Creating delicious desserts is challenging, fun and rewarding. And since desserts often command more compliments than the main course, the time and effort spent on them is well worthwhile.

Choosing the right dessert to complement a meal is important. Fresh, fruity desserts are apt finishes for summer meals. They are cool and refreshing and usually quick to prepare. Light and frothy whips and soufflés round off rich meals. And elaborate, creamy concoctions are delicious after a lighter main course. Pies, puddings and cakes will satisfy robust appetites, especially in the cold winter months.

Ice cream and frozen desserts are, perhaps, the most versatile of all desserts. They can, of course, be prepared well in advance and are wonderful to have on hand when unexpected guests arrive. They can be as light and fresh as a fruit sherbet or as creamy rich as Bombe Grand Marnier.

Most desserts can be prepared ahead of time and need just a little attention at the last minute – a point worth remembering, whether you're cooking for a hungry family or giving a special dinner party.

NOTES:

Always preheat the oven to the specified temperature.

Margarine can be substituted for butter in all recipes. For better flavor in baking, use unsalted butter if possible.

All recipes have been tested with large eggs.

When measuring flour for baking, spoon lightly into the measuring cup, then level with a knife or spatula. Don't dip the measuring cup directly into the flour – it can result in heavy baked goods. Measure flour unsifted unless stated otherwise.

SOUFFLÉS, MOUSSES & CHARLOTTES

Rich Chocolate Mousse

3 oz semisweet chocolate
3 eggs, separated
2 tablespoons sherry

Melt the chocolate in the top of a double boiler over hot water. Beat in the egg yolks and sherry; let cool.

Beat the egg whites until peaks form; gently fold into the chocolate. Pour into individual ramekins and refrigerate until set. Top with whipped cream and chocolate curls.

4 servings

Orange Mousse

- 2 envelopes unflavored gelatin
- Grated rind and juice of 1 lemon
- 1 can (6 oz) frozen orange juice concentrate, thawed
- 4 eggs
- 2 egg yolks
- ½ cup sugar
- ¾ cup whipping cream, whipped

Stir the gelatin with the lemon juice in a small saucepan. Add the orange juice and warm, stirring, until the gelatin dissolves. Cool slightly.

Beat the eggs, egg yolks, sugar and lemon rind in a mixer bowl until thick. Fold in the whipped cream, then the gelatin mixture. Pour into a serving bowl and refrigerate until set.

To serve, pipe additional whipped cream around the mousse and garnish with orange rind.

6 to 8 servings

Strawberry Mousse

1 pint strawberries
2 envelopes unflavored gelatin
¼ cup orange juice
2 eggs
1 egg yolk
½ cup sugar
1½ cups whipping cream, whipped

Set aside several strawberries to decorate the mousse. Puree the remainder in a blender.

Stir the gelatin into the orange juice in a small metal bowl. Set the bowl in hot water until the gelatin dissolves. Cool slightly.

Combine the eggs, egg yolk and sugar in a mixer bowl and beat until thick. Fold in the gelatin mixture, the strawberry puree and the whipped cream. Pour into a 4-cup ring mold. Refrigerate until set.

Unmold on a serving dish. Decorate the mousse with whipped cream and the reserved strawberries.

8 servings

Chocolate-Orange Mousse

- 8 oz semisweet chocolate
- 6 tablespoons milk
- 2 envelopes unflavored gelatin
- Grated rind and juice of 1 orange
- 4 eggs
- 2 egg yolks
- ½ cup sugar
- 1 cup whipping cream, whipped

Combine the chocolate and milk in a small saucepan and heat slowly until melted. Let cool.

Stir the gelatin into the orange juice in a small metal bowl. Set the bowl in hot water until the gelatin dissolves. Cool slightly.

Beat the eggs, egg yolks, sugar and orange rind in a mixer bowl until thick. Stir in the cooled chocolate and gelatin mixtures. Beat over a bowl of ice until slightly thickened. Gently fold in the whipped cream. Spoon into a serving bowl or individual dessert dishes. Refrigerate until set.

Serve garnished with additional whipped cream and chocolate curls.

6 to 8 servings

Coffee and Praline Mousse

- 1 envelope unflavored gelatin
- ¼ cup strong coffee
- 3 eggs
- 2 egg yolks
- ½ cup sugar
- 1½ cups whipping cream, whipped
- ½ cup crushed praline (page 46)

CARAMEL:

- ½ cup sugar
- ¼ cup water
- ¼ cup strong black coffee

First make the caramel. Dissolve the sugar in the water in a small saucepan over low heat, then boil until it turns a rich brown. Remove from the heat. Add the hot coffee carefully (it splatters) all at once, stirring until thoroughly blended. If necessary, return to the heat to warm and melt the caramel; cool.

Stir the gelatin into the coffee in a small metal bowl. Set the bowl in hot water until the gelatin dissolves. Cool slightly.

Beat the eggs, egg yolks and sugar in a mixer bowl until thick. Fold in the gelatin, the whipped cream and the caramel. Stir gently over a bowl of ice until thickened. Stir in the praline.

Pour into an oiled 6-cup mold and refrigerate until set.

Carefully unmold on a serving dish. Serve with cream.

8 servings

Chocolate Chestnut Mold

- 8 oz semisweet chocolate
- 5 tablespoons milk
- ½ cup butter
- ½ cup sugar
- 2 cans (8 oz each) unsweetened chestnut puree
- 3 tablespoons brandy

Combine the chocolate and milk in a small saucepan and heat gently until melted. Let cool.

Cream the butter and sugar in a mixer bowl until light and fluffy. Add the chestnut puree a little at a time, beating well after each addition. Stir in the melted chocolate and the brandy. Pour into an oiled 4-cup mold. Refrigerate overnight.

Carefully unmold on a serving dish. Garnish with whipped cream.

8 servings

Mocha Charlotte

- 6 oz semisweet chocolate
- 2 cups strong black coffee
- 2 eggs, separated
- ¼ cup sugar
- 2 envelopes unflavored gelatin, softened in ¼ cup water
- 1⅓ cups whipping cream, whipped

Melt the chocolate in ¾ cup of the coffee over low heat. Add the remaining coffee and bring to a boil, stirring. Remove from the heat.

Beat the egg yolks and sugar until creamy. Stir in the coffee mixture. Return to the saucepan and stir over low heat until the mixture thickens. Add the gelatin and stir until dissolved. Let cool.

Stir over a bowl of ice until the mixture starts to thicken; fold in the whipped cream. Beat the egg whites until stiff; fold into the mixture. Pour into an oiled 1½-quart charlotte mold; refrigerate until set.

Unmold on a serving plate. If desired, spread additional whipped cream on the side; press in cookies or ladyfingers. Pipe whipped cream on top and center with grated chocolate.

6 to 8 servings

Charlotte Russe

6 egg yolks
¾ cup sugar
2 cups milk
1 teaspoon vanilla
2 envelopes unflavored gelatin, softened in ¼ cup water
2 cups whipping cream, whipped
12 ladyfingers, split

Beat the egg yolks and sugar until smooth. Bring the milk just to the boiling point. Remove from the heat and stir in the vanilla. Gradually pour in the egg mixture, stirring vigorously with a wire whisk. Pour the mixture into the top of a double boiler and heat over simmering water, stirring, until thickened. Add the gelatin and stir until dissolved. Let cool.

Fold the whipped cream into the custard. Line a 1½-quart charlotte mold with the ladyfingers, cut sides in. Trim the ends evenly with the top of the mold. Make a flower pattern in the bottom of the mold with the ladyfinger trimmings. Pour the custard into the mold and refrigerate until set.

Unmold on a serving dish. Garnish with additional whipped cream and, if desired, decorate with a glacé cherry and angelica.

8 servings

Cold Lime Soufflé

- 6 eggs, separated
- 1 cup superfine sugar
- Grated rind of 1 lime
- Juice of 3 limes
- 1 envelope unflavored gelatin, softened in ¼ cup water
- Green food coloring (optional)
- 1½ cups whipping cream, whipped
- ¼ teaspoon cream of tartar
- ¼ cup chopped toasted almonds

Beat the egg yolks and sugar together in a mixing bowl until smooth. Stir in the lime rind and juice and mix thoroughly. Pour the mixture into the top of a double boiler and heat over simmering water until thick, stirring occasionally. Add the gelatin mixture and food coloring and warm, stirring, until dissolved. Let cool. Refrigerate until the mixture is thickened but not yet set around the side of the bowl.

Fold the whipped cream into the lime mixture. Beat the egg whites with the cream of tartar until stiff and fold into the lime mixture.

Fold a long strip of waxed paper into thirds and secure around a 2-quart soufflé dish to form a collar that stands 2 inches above the rim. Butter the inside of the collar. Spoon the lime mixture into the dish and refrigerate until set.

Carefully remove the collar and press the chopped almonds around the side of the soufflé. Garnish the top of the soufflé with additional whipped cream.

8 to 10 servings

Chilled Lemon Soufflé

- 3 large eggs, separated
- 3/4 cup sugar
- Grated rind and juice of 2 lemons
- 1 1/3 cups whipping cream, whipped
- 2 envelopes unflavored gelatin
- 1/4 cup water
- 2 tablespoons chopped toasted almonds

Combine the egg yolks, sugar and lemon rind in a mixer bowl. Heat the lemon juice and beat into the egg mixture until thick. Fold in the whipped cream.

Stir the gelatin into the water in a small metal bowl. Set the bowl in hot water until the gelatin dissolves. Stir into the lemon mixture and cool until almost set.

Meanwhile, fold a long strip of waxed paper into thirds and secure around a 3-cup soufflé dish to form a collar that stands 2 inches above the rim. Butter the inside of the collar. Beat the egg whites until stiff; fold into the lemon mixture. Spoon into the dish and chill until set.

Carefully remove the collar and press the nuts around the sides. Garnish with whipped cream if desired.

6 to 8 servings

Soufflé Omelet

- 4 eggs, separated
- 2 tablespoons light cream
- 1 tablespoon granulated sugar
- 1 tablespoon butter
- 3 tablespoons strawberry jam
- Powdered sugar

Beat the egg yolks, cream and granulated sugar with a wire whisk. Beat the egg whites until stiff; fold into the yolks.

Melt the butter in an 8-inch omelet pan. Pour in the eggs and spread evenly. Cook the omelet over moderate heat for 2 minutes, until golden brown underneath.

Place the pan in a 400° oven and bake for 3 minutes, until the top is set. Warm the jam.

Remove the omelet from the oven and quickly spread with the jam. Fold in half with a spatula and slide onto a warmed serving dish. Sprinkle with the powdered sugar. Heat the tines of a kitchen fork and score a lattice pattern on the top. Serve immediately.

2 servings

CREAMS, CUSTARDS & PUDDINGS

Banana Whip

- 1 egg white
- 2 tablespoons sugar
- 4 ripe bananas, mashed
- ¾ cup whipping cream, whipped

Beat the egg white until stiff. Beat in the sugar. Fold the egg white and the mashed bananas into the whipped cream.

Spoon into individual dessert dishes and serve immediately. Accompany with cookies.

4 to 6 servings

Raspberry Cream

- 1 package (10 oz) frozen raspberries, thawed
- 1 cup whipping cream, whipped

Puree the raspberries and their juice in a blender until smooth. Strain into a mixing bowl and fold in the whipped cream. Spoon into individual dessert dishes and chill. Serve with cookies.
6 servings

Creamy Rice Pudding

- ½ cup rice
- 2½ cups milk
- 2 tablespoons sugar
- ¼ teaspoon vanilla
- ¾ cup whipping cream, whipped

APRICOT SAUCE:

- ⅔ cup dried apricots, soaked overnight in 2 cups water
- ½ cup sugar
- 2 teaspoons lemon juice

Combine the rice and milk in a saucepan and bring to a boil, stirring constantly. Reduce the heat and simmer gently for 40 minutes, adding extra milk if necessary. Stir in the 2 tablespoons sugar and the vanilla and pour into a mixing bowl to cool. Fold in the whipped cream and chill until cold.

Prepare the apricot sauce. Simmer the apricots in their soaking water for 15 minutes. Cool slightly. Puree in a blender until smooth. Stir in the sugar and lemon juice and keep warm.

Serve the warm apricot sauce over the chilled pudding.

4 to 6 servings

Zabaglione

- 4 egg yolks
- ½ cup sugar
- ¼ cup Marsala wine

Combine the egg yolks, sugar and Marsala in the top of a double boiler and whisk together over simmering water until very thick.

Pour into individual dessert glasses. Serve immediately, with ladyfingers if desired.

4 servings

Prune Whip

- 1½ cups pitted prunes
- ¾ cup yogurt
- 2 tablespoons honey
- 1¼ cups whipping cream, whipped
- 2 tablespoons chopped walnuts

Place the prunes in a saucepan with just enough water to cover and simmer for 15 minutes, until tender. Drain, reserving ½ cup of the cooking liquid. Puree the prunes and reserved cooking liquid in a blender. Let cool.

Combine the puree, yogurt and honey in a bowl and fold in the whipped cream. Spoon into individual dessert dishes and sprinkle with the walnuts.

6 to 8 servings

Peach Bavarian

- 2 cups finely chopped peaches
- Juice of 1 lemon
- ½ cup sugar
- 1 envelope unflavored gelatin
- ½ cup water
- ½ teaspoon each vanilla and almond extract
- 1½ cups whipping cream, whipped

Toss the peaches in the lemon juice and sugar; let stand for 1 hour. Stir the gelatin into the water in a small metal bowl. Set in hot water until the gelatin dissolves. Stir in the peaches. Refrigerate until just beginning to thicken. Stir the vanilla and almond extract into the peach mixture; fold in the whipped cream. Spoon into individual ramekins and chill until set. Garnish with additional cream and peach wedges.

6 servings

Peach Brûlée

- 6 fresh peaches, peeled, halved and pitted
- 2 tablespoons Cointreau
- 1¼ cups whipping cream, whipped
- ⅔ cup packed brown sugar

Place the peach halves in a shallow ovenproof dish and sprinkle with the Cointreau.

Spread the cream over the peaches, covering them completely. Sprinkle with the sugar. Brown under a hot broiler for 3 minutes. Let cool, then chill before serving.

6 servings

Sherry Trifle

- 1 sponge cake (8 inch), sliced
- 3 tablespoons jam
- 3 egg yolks
- 2 teaspoons cornstarch
- 2 tablespoons sugar
- 2 cups milk
- 5 tablespoons sherry
- 2 bananas, sliced
- 3/4 cup whipping cream, whipped

Spread the cake slices with the jam and arrange in the bottom of a glass serving bowl.

Beat the egg yolks, cornstarch and sugar until smooth. Bring the milk to a boil in a saucepan. Remove from the heat and stir a few spoonfuls into the egg mixture. Pour the egg mixture into the milk and return to low heat. Simmer, stirring, until the mixture is thick enough to coat a spoon. Cool.

Sprinkle the sherry over the cake. Top with a layer of bananas. Pour the custard over; let set. Spread whipped cream on top; pipe rosettes around the edge if desired. Garnish with glacé cherries and toasted almonds.

4 servings

Pots de Chocolat

4 oz semisweet chocolate
2½ cups milk
2 eggs
2 egg yolks
¼ cup sugar

Warm the chocolate and milk in a saucepan over low heat to melt the chocolate. Beat the eggs, egg yolks and sugar together and stir into the chocolate mixture.

Strain into individual ovenproof crème pots or ramekins. Place in a roasting pan with 1 inch of water. Bake in a 350° oven for 35 to 40 minutes, until just set. Cool, then refrigerate. Serve cold.

4 to 6 servings

Creamy Lemon Whip

- Grated rind and juice of 1 lemon
- ½ cup white wine
- ½ cup sugar
- 1½ cups whipping cream
- 1 egg white

Combine the lemon rind and juice, wine and half the sugar in a bowl and let stand for 1 hour.

Whip the cream until it begins to thicken. Gradually add the wine mixture and continue beating until the cream holds its shape.

Beat the egg white until stiff; beat in the remaining sugar. Carefully fold into the whipped cream mixture. Spoon into individual dessert dishes and serve.

4 servings

Scotch Whip

- 1/3 cup chopped almonds
- 1/4 cup rolled oats
- 1 1/2 cups whipping cream
- 1 tablespoon lemon juice
- 5 tablespoons Scotch whiskey
- 1/4 cup honey

Spread the almonds and oats on a baking sheet and brown under the broiler, turning frequently. Let cool.

Whip the cream until it stands in soft peaks. Beat in the lemon juice, Scotch and honey. Fold in the browned almonds and oats. Spoon into dessert glasses and refrigerate.

Serve garnished with lemon twists.

6 servings

Apricot Ambrosia

- 1 can (17 oz) apricot halves, drained
- 1 tablespoon honey
- 8 coconut macaroons
- 3/4 cup whipping cream, whipped
- 1 tablespoon sliced almonds

Puree the apricots with the honey in a blender.

Break the macaroons into bite-size pieces. Fold the apricot puree and the macaroon pieces into the whipped cream. Spoon into individual dessert dishes and chill.

Serve cold, sprinkled with the almonds.

4 servings

Crème Caramel

- 1/2 cup sugar
- 3 tablespoons water
- 3 eggs
- 2 cups milk
- 1/2 teaspoon vanilla

Combine 6 tablespoons of the sugar and the water in a small saucepan and heat gently, stirring, until the sugar dissolves. Cook, without stirring, to a rich caramel. Carefully stir in 1 teaspoon boiling water. Pour the caramel into a 1-quart mold. Let set.

Beat the eggs with the remaining sugar. Heat the milk almost to boiling; stir into the egg mixture along with the vanilla. Mix well. Strain into the mold. Place in a roasting pan filled with 1 inch of water. Bake in a 275° oven for 1 1/2 hours, or until set. Cool. Unmold on a serving dish.

4 servings

Raisin Bread Pudding

- 6 slices white bread, crusts removed
- ½ teaspoon ground cinnamon
- ¼ teaspoon grated nutmeg
- ½ cup raisins
- 4 eggs
- ½ cup sugar
- 2½ cups milk

Cut each slice of bread into quarters. Arrange half the pieces in the bottom of a greased 1½-quart casserole. Sprinkle with half the spices and raisins and top with the remaining bread, spices and raisins.

Beat the eggs and sugar together until smooth. Add the milk and beat until well blended. Pour over the bread and let stand for 1 hour.

Place the casserole in a roasting pan filled with 1 inch of water. Bake in a 350° oven for 55 to 65 minutes, or until a knife inserted in the center comes out clean.

Serve warm, with heavy cream.

6 to 8 servings

Indian Pudding

- 3½ cups milk
- ½ cup cornmeal
- ¼ cup packed brown sugar
- ¼ cup granulated sugar
- ¼ cup molasses
- ½ teaspoon salt
- 4 tablespoons butter
- ½ teaspoon ground cinnamon
- ¼ teaspoon grated nutmeg

Heat the milk to scalding in a large saucepan; reduce heat. Slowly sprinkle the cornmeal into the milk, stirring constantly. Simmer over low heat for 20 minutes, stirring occasionally.

Add the remaining ingredients and stir well. Pour into a buttered 5-cup soufflé dish or casserole. Bake in a 325° oven for 1½ to 2 hours, or until set.

Serve warm, topped with ice cream.

6 to 8 servings

Lemon Pudding

- 4 tablespoons butter
- Grated rind and juice of 1 large lemon
- ½ cup sugar
- 2 eggs, separated
- ¼ cup all-purpose flour
- ¾ cup milk

Cream the butter with the lemon rind and sugar until light and fluffy. Mix in the egg yolks, flour and lemon juice. Gradually stir in the milk. Beat the egg whites until stiff and carefully fold into the mixture.

Pour into a buttered 1-quart baking dish and place in a roasting pan filled with 1 inch of water.

Bake in a 350° oven for 40 to 45 minutes, until set and golden brown. Serve warm.

4 to 6 servings

Rhubarb Crumble

- 6 tablespoons butter
- 1¾ cups whole wheat flour
- ½ cup packed brown sugar
- 1½ lb rhubarb, cut into 1-inch pieces
- ½ cup granulated sugar

Combine the butter and flour and work the mixture with a fork until it resembles coarse crumbs. Stir in the brown sugar.

Arrange a layer of rhubarb in the bottom of a 1-quart baking dish and sprinkle with granulated sugar. Continue layering rhubarb and sugar until both are used up. Cover the fruit completely with the crumble mixture. Bake in a 350° oven for 40 to 50 minutes, or until crisp and golden brown. Serve hot or cold.

4 to 6 servings

Bread and Butter Pudding

4 tablespoons butter
6 slices white bread, crusts removed
⅓ cup raisins
¼ cup sugar
2 large eggs
2½ cups milk
Grated nutmeg

Generously butter each slice of bread and cut into quarters. Arrange half the bread pieces, buttered sides down, in a 1½-quart baking dish. Sprinkle with the raisins and half the sugar. Cover with the remaining bread pieces, buttered sides up.

Beat the eggs and milk together and pour over the bread. Sprinkle with the remaining sugar and the nutmeg. Let stand for 30 minutes.

Bake in a 325° oven for 50 to 60 minutes, until the top is golden brown. Serve with cream.

4 servings

Apricot Upside-Down Cake

- 1 cup butter
- ¾ cup packed brown sugar
- 1 can (17 oz) apricot halves
- ¾ cup granulated sugar
- 3 eggs
- 1½ cups all-purpose flour
- 2¼ teaspoons baking powder
- ½ teaspoon salt
- 1 teaspoon ground allspice

Melt 4 tablespoons of the butter and mix with the brown sugar. Spread over the bottom of a 9-inch round layer pan. Reserve 3 tablespoons of the apricot juice; drain the remaining juice from the fruit. Arrange the apricot halves, cut sides down, in the pan.

Cream the remaining butter with the granulated sugar until light and fluffy. Add the eggs, one at a time, stirring in a little of the flour with the last two eggs. Fold in the remaining flour, the baking powder, salt, allspice and reserved apricot juice.

Spread the batter over the apricots. Bake in a 350° oven for 55 to 60 minutes, or until the cake springs back when pressed lightly.

Invert onto a warmed serving dish and serve with cream.

6 servings

Crisp Apple Bake

- 6 tablespoons butter
- 10 slices white bread, crusts removed
- 1½ to 2 lb apples, peeled and sliced
- ½ cup packed brown sugar

Generously butter each slice of bread and cut into quarters.

Line the bottom of a buttered 1½-quart baking dish with a third of the bread, buttered sides down. Cover with half the apples and a third of the sugar.

Arrange another layer of the bread on top, cover with the remaining apples and half of the remaining sugar. Cover with the remaining bread, buttered sides up and slightly overlapping to form a pattern. Sprinkle with the last of the sugar.

Cover with foil and bake in a 350° oven for 35 minutes. Remove the foil and bake 5 minutes, or until the bread is golden brown.

Serve hot, with cream.

6 servings

FRUIT DESSERTS

Tropical Fruit Salad

1 small ripe pineapple
1 can (11 oz) lychees, drained
2 bananas, sliced
1 guava or papaya, peeled, seeded and sliced
2 passion fruits (optional)
1 cup ginger ale

Cut the pineapple in half lengthwise; remove and discard the core and cut the flesh into cubes. Place in a serving bowl with the lychees and sliced bananas and guava.

Halve the passion fruits, scoop out the flesh and mix with the other fruit. Toss the fruit with the ginger ale and chill. Serve with cream if desired.

8 servings

Bananas Flambé

4 bananas, halved lengthwise
½ cup packed brown sugar
2 tablespoons lemon juice
2 tablespoons butter
2 tablespoons rum

Arrange the bananas in one layer in a baking dish and sprinkle with the sugar and lemon juice. Dot with the butter and bake in a 350° oven for 15 minutes.

Transfer the bananas to a warmed serving dish. Spoon the sauce over them.

Warm the rum. Pour it over the bananas and carefully ignite; serve flaming. Accompany with cream if desired.

4 servings

Peaches in Blueberry Sauce

1 pint blueberries, crushed
¼ cup sugar
1 tablespoon lemon juice
½ teaspoon vanilla
6 peaches, peeled

Combine the blueberries, sugar and lemon juice in a saucepan. Bring to a boil and boil for 1 minute, stirring constantly to avoid burning. Cool slightly, then puree in a blender. Strain through a fine sieve and then add the vanilla.

Place the peaches in a serving bowl. Pour the blueberry sauce over them. Chill thoroughly.

Serve with cream if desired.

6 servings

Baked Stuffed Apples

- 4 large apples
- 1/4 cup chopped dates
- 1/4 cup raisins
- 1/4 cup packed brown sugar
- 1/2 teaspoon ground cinnamon
- 1 tablespoon butter

Core the apples. Make a cut around the circumference of each apple at its widest point.

Combine the dates, raisins, sugar and cinnamon. Divide between the apples, spooning the mixture into the cores.

Dot each apple with a little butter and place in a baking dish. Bake in a 350° oven for 50 to 60 minutes, until tender. Serve hot, with cream.

4 servings

Red Fruit Compote

- 1 cup sugar
- 1 1/4 cups water
- 1 lb Bing cherries, pitted
- Grated rind and juice of 1/2 orange
- 1 pint strawberries
- 1 pint blackberries
- 1 pint raspberries
- 1 1/2 tablespoons arrowroot
- 2 tablespoons port
- Crémets (opposite)

Combine the sugar and water in a saucepan and cook gently, stirring, until the sugar dissolves. Increase the heat, bring to a boil and boil for a few minutes. Add the cherries and orange rind; simmer for 5 minutes, until soft.

Remove the cherries from the syrup with a slotted spoon and transfer to a serving dish. Add the remaining fruit to the syrup and bring to a boil. Blend the arrowroot with the orange juice and stir into the boiling syrup. Boil, stirring, until thickened. Add the port. Pour the syrup over the fruit. Cool before serving. Serve with crémets.

8 servings

Calvados Apples

- 1 cup sugar
- 1 1/2 cups water
- 6 apples, peeled and quartered
- 1/4 cup Calvados or brandy

Place 2/3 cup of the sugar and 1 1/4 cups of the water in a large saucepan and simmer, stirring, until the sugar dissolves. Bring to a boil; reduce heat and simmer for 5 minutes. Place the apples in the syrup, cover and simmer for 15 to 20 minutes. Let cool. Remove the apples from the syrup and place in a serving dish. Increase the heat and boil the syrup rapidly until reduced by half. Add the Calvados and pour over the apples; let cool.

Place the remaining sugar and water in a saucepan and heat gently, stirring, until dissolved. Increase the heat and boil rapidly until golden brown. Pour onto a greased baking sheet and let harden. When set, crack into pieces and sprinkle over the apples. Serve with cookies if desired.

4 servings

Crémets

1 cup cream-style cottage cheese
2 tablespoons sugar
1 cup whipping cream

Combine the cottage cheese with the sugar. Gradually beat in the cream. Spoon into a serving dish and chill. Serve with stewed fruit.

Makes about 2 cups

Winter Fruit Salad

- 1 cup dried apricots, soaked overnight
- ¾ cup dried prunes, soaked overnight
- ¾ cup dried figs, soaked overnight
- 2 tablespoons honey
- 1-inch piece of cinnamon stick
- 2 cloves
- Juice of ½ lemon
- ½ cup raisins
- ¼ cup coarsely chopped walnuts
- 2 tablespoons toasted slivered almonds

Drain the dried fruits, reserving 2½ cups of their liquid or adding enough water to equal that amount. Combine the liquid in a saucepan with the honey, cinnamon stick and cloves; bring to a boil. Add the lemon juice. Add the dried fruits to the pan, cover and simmer over low heat for 10 minutes. Add the raisins and simmer for 2 to 3 minutes longer.

Discard the cinnamon stick. Spoon the fruit into a serving dish and sprinkle with the walnuts and almonds. Serve warm or cold, with cream if desired.

6 servings

Molded Fruit Salad

- 3¼ cups water
- 1 cup sugar
- Grated rind and juice of 3 lemons
- 1-inch piece of cinnamon stick
- 3 envelopes unflavored gelatin, softened in ½ cup water
- ¼ cup sherry
- ½ lb seedless green grapes
- ½ lb seedless red grapes
- Whipped cream

Combine the water, sugar, lemon rind and juice and cinnamon stick in a large saucepan. Heat gently, stirring, until sugar is dissolved. Add the gelatin mixture and stir until dissolved. Add the sherry. Let cool slightly. Strain, discarding the lemon rind and the cinnamon stick.

Reserve a few of the green grapes to decorate the mold. Pour a small amount of the gelatin mixture into a 5-cup ring mold and refrigerate until set. Arrange some of the red grapes on the set gelatin and pour in enough gelatin to cover; refrigerate until set. Add another layer of gelatin and let set. Arrange green grapes on top. Continue in this manner until the mold is filled. Refrigerate until set.

Invert onto a serving platter and unmold. Garnish with whipped cream and the reserved grapes.

8 to 10 servings

Pineapple Romanoff

- 1 large pineapple
- ½ cup powdered sugar
- Grated rind of ½ orange
- ¼ cup Curaçao or Cointreau
- 1 pint strawberries
- 1½ cups whipping cream, whipped with ¼ cup sugar

Cut the pineapple in half lengthwise. Cut out and discard the core. Scoop out the flesh and cut into cubes. Reserve the shells.

Combine the pineapple, powdered sugar, orange rind and Curaçao in a bowl and let soak for 2 hours.

Reserve a few strawberries for decoration and slice the remainder. Fold the marinated pineapple and the strawberries into the whipped cream.

Spoon into the pineapple shells. Decorate with the reserved strawberries and refrigerate for 30 minutes before serving.

4 to 6 servings

Pavlova

- 4 egg whites
- 1 1/4 cups sugar
- 1 tablespoon cornstarch
- 2 teaspoons white vinegar
- 1/4 teaspoon vanilla
- 1 1/2 cups whipping cream
- 2 bananas, sliced
- 1 small pineapple, cut into cubes
- 2 peaches, peeled and sliced
- 2 passion fruits, peeled and sliced (optional)

Beat the egg whites until foamy. Add 1 cup of the sugar, 2 tablespoons at a time, beating until the mixture is very stiff. Beat in the cornstarch, vinegar and vanilla.

Spoon the meringue onto a baking sheet lined with brown wrapping paper, and form into a 9-inch round. Hollow out the center slightly. Bake in a 200° oven for 1 1/2 hours. Let cool.

Whip the cream with the remaining sugar until stiff. Reserve some of the fruit for decorating; fold the remaining fruit into the cream. Spoon the mixture into the center of the meringue. Decorate with the reserved fruit.

6 to 8 servings

Pears Poached in Wine

6 Bosc pears
⅔ cup sugar
⅔ cup water
⅔ cup dry red wine
1-inch piece of
 cinnamon stick
2 teaspoons
 arrowroot

Leaving the stems on, peel the pears. Combine the sugar, water, wine and cinnamon stick in a saucepan. Heat gently until the sugar dissolves. Increase the heat, bring to a boil and boil for 5 minutes.

Place the pears in the syrup. Cover and simmer for 20 to 30 minutes, until tender. Arrange the pears on a serving dish.

Remove and discard the cinnamon stick. Mix the arrowroot with a little water. Add to the syrup and bring to a boil, stirring constantly. Simmer, stirring, for 1 minute. Let cool. Spoon over the pears and refrigerate until serving time.

6 servings

Oranges in Caramel Sauce

Finely shredded rind of 1 orange
8 oranges, peeled
1 cup sugar
½ cup cold water
⅔ cup hot water

Blanch the orange rind in boiling water for 1 minute; drain and pat dry. Remove any pith from the oranges and slice thinly. Arrange in four individual dessert dishes.

Combine the sugar and cold water in a saucepan. Heat gently until dissolved. Increase the heat and boil steadily to a rich brown caramel. Carefully pour in the hot water (it splatters) and heat, stirring, for 1 minute. Let cool.

Pour the caramel over the oranges, sprinkle with the orange rind and refrigerate. Serve chilled. Accompany with cookies if desired.

4 servings

FROZEN DESSERTS

Lemon-Orange Ice Cream

- 3 eggs, separated
- ¾ cup sugar
- Grated rind and juice of 1 lemon
- Grated rind and juice of 1 orange
- 1½ cups whipping cream, whipped

Beat the egg yolks, half the sugar and the lemon and orange rinds in a large mixer bowl until thick. Pour the fruit juices into a saucepan and heat gently. Pour into the egg mixture and beat over hot water until thick. Remove from the heat.

Beat the egg whites until stiff. Beat in the remaining sugar. Fold into the fruit mixture. Fold in the whipped cream. Spoon into a freezer container; cover tightly and freeze until firm.

Spoon into chilled dessert glasses to serve.

6 to 8 servings

Frozen Mocha Mousse

- 2 oz semisweet chocolate
- 1 tablespoon instant coffee
- 2 tablespoons water
- 3 eggs, separated
- ½ cup sugar
- ¾ cup whipping cream, whipped

Place the chocolate, coffee and water in the top of a double boiler and heat gently until melted; let cool. Beat the egg yolks and sugar in a mixer bowl until thick and creamy.

Beat the melted chocolate mixture into the egg mixture, then fold in the whipped cream.

Beat the egg whites until stiff; carefully fold into the chocolate mixture. Pour into individual ramekins. Cover and freeze 3 to 4 hours.

Ten minutes before serving, transfer to the refrigerator to soften. Decorate with chocolate curls.

4 to 6 servings.

Vanilla Ice Cream

- 2 eggs
- 2 egg yolks
- ½ cup sugar
- 2 cups milk or half-and-half
- ⅛ teaspoon vanilla
- 1½ cups whipping cream, whipped

Beat the eggs, egg yolks and sugar together in a mixer bowl. Slowly bring the milk to a boil in a saucepan. Beat into the egg mixture. Blend in the vanilla and let cool. Gently fold in the whipped cream.

Pour into a freezer container; cover and freeze for 1 hour. Stir well, then return to the freezer until firm. Twenty minutes before serving, transfer to the refrigerator to soften. Spoon into chilled dishes. Serve with cookies if desired.

8 servings

Chocolate: Melt 8 oz semisweet chocolate with the milk and proceed as directed.

Praline: Combine ½ cup blanched almonds and ¼ cup sugar in a saucepan; heat gently until the sugar melts. Boil until the mixture turns nut brown. Pour onto a greased baking sheet in a thin layer and let set. Crush with a rolling pin or wooden mallet. Fold in with the whipped cream.

Coffee: Dissolve 3 tablespoons instant coffee in 2 tablespoons boiling water; cool. Add with the whipped cream.

Ginger: Add ½ cup finely chopped preserved stem ginger to the eggs and sugar. Add 2 tablespoons of the syrup from the preserves with the whipped cream.

Banana Milk Ice

1 can (13 oz) evaporated milk, chilled
⅔ cup packed brown sugar
3 ripe bananas
1 tablespoon lemon juice

Beat the evaporated milk in a mixer bowl until very thick. Beat in the sugar. Mash the bananas with the lemon juice and beat into the evaporated milk.

Pour into a freezer container; cover and freeze for 1 hour. Stir well, then return to the freezer until firm.

Thirty minutes before serving, transfer to the refrigerator to soften. Spoon into chilled dishes.

6 to 8 servings

Strawberry Ice Cream

1 pint strawberries
2 envelopes unflavored gelatin
¼ cup cold water
1 can (13 oz) evaporated milk, chilled
¾ cup sugar
Juice of ½ lemon

Puree the strawberries in a blender until smooth. Strain to remove the seeds.

Stir the gelatin into the water in a small metal bowl. Set in hot water until the gelatin dissolves. Combine with the strawberry puree.

Beat the evaporated milk until thick. Stir in the sugar, lemon juice and the strawberry puree. Pour into a freezer container; cover and freeze for 1 hour. Stir well. Return to the freezer until firm.

Twenty minutes before serving, transfer to the refrigerator to soften. Spoon into chilled dessert glasses and garnish each with a strawberry.

8 servings

Pineapple Ice Cream

1 large ripe pineapple
3 egg whites
¾ cup sugar
1½ cups whipping cream, whipped

Cut the pineapple in half lengthwise. Remove and discard the core. Scoop the flesh and juice into a bowl. Chill the shells. Finely chop the flesh.

Beat the egg whites until stiff. Gradually beat in the sugar, then fold in the whipped cream and the chopped pineapple and juice.

Pour into a freezer container; cover and freeze for 1 hour. Stir well. Return to the freezer until firm.

Twenty minutes before serving, transfer to the refrigerator to soften. Spoon into the chilled pineapple shells and arrange on a serving platter, or spoon into chilled individual dessert dishes.

6 to 8 servings

Bombe Noël

- ⅓ cup each chopped candied cherries, angelica, pineapple and ginger
- ⅓ cup raisins
- 2 tablespoons each brandy and Cointreau
- 3 egg yolks
- ½ cup sugar
- 1½ cups half-and-half
- ⅛ teaspoon vanilla
- ¾ cup whipping cream, whipped

Combine the candied cherries, angelica, pineapple and ginger and the raisins in a bowl. Pour the brandy and Cointreau over and soak for 1 hour.

Beat the egg yolks and sugar in a mixer bowl until creamy. Bring the half-and-half to a boil slowly in a saucepan. Beat into the egg mixture. Stir in the vanilla and let cool.

Fold the fruit and whipped cream into the custard; cover and freeze for 1 hour. Stir well. Pour into a 1½-quart metal mold; cover with foil and freeze until firm.

To unmold, dip the bottom of the mold into cold water and invert onto a chilled platter; remove mold. Garnish with additional whipped cream, candied angelica and pineapple.

6 to 8 servings

Biscuit Tortoni

½ cup ground almonds
1¼ cups amaretti biscuit crumbs
1½ cups half-and-half
1 teaspoon vanilla
½ cup sugar
3 tablespoons rum
2 cups whipping cream, whipped

Combine the ground almonds and 1 cup of the amaretti crumbs in a mixing bowl. Stir in the half-and-half and vanilla; let soak for 30 minutes. Stir in the sugar and rum. Spoon into a freezer container. Freeze until ice crystals form around the side.

Remove from the freezer and fold in the whipped cream. Spoon into individual freezer dishes and cover with plastic wrap. Freeze until firm.

Ten minutes before serving, transfer to the refrigerator to soften. Sprinkle with the remaining amaretti crumbs.
6 to 8 servings

Blackberry Ice Cream

- 1 pint blackberries
- 6 tablespoons sugar
- ½ cup water
- 3 egg yolks
- 2 cups half-and-half
- 2 tablespoons powdered sugar

Simmer the blackberries in a saucepan with 2 tablespoons of the sugar for about 10 minutes. Puree in a blender and strain to remove the seeds.

Combine the water and remaining sugar in a saucepan and warm, stirring, until the sugar dissolves. Increase the heat and boil steadily, covered, for 5 minutes without stirring.

Cool the syrup slightly, then beat into the egg yolks until the mixture is thick.

Combine the half-and-half, blackberry puree and powdered sugar and fold into the beaten egg mixture. Pour into a freezer container; cover and freeze until firm.

Twenty minutes before serving, transfer to the refrigerator to soften. Spoon into chilled dessert glasses. Serve with cookies if desired. For a special touch, pass blackberry brandy for guests to garnish their ice cream.

8 servings

Pineapple Granita

- 1 large pineapple
- ¾ cup sugar
- 2 cups water
- 1 egg white

Cut the pineapple in half lengthwise. Remove and discard the core. Scoop out the flesh and juice and puree in a blender. Chill the shells.

Combine the sugar and water in a saucepan and heat gently, stirring, until dissolved. Stir in the pineapple puree and mix well. Pour into a freezer container; cover and freeze for 3 hours, until partially frozen.

Beat the egg white until stiff; fold into the partially frozen ice. Cover and freeze until firm.

Ten minutes before serving, transfer to the refrigerator. Scoop into the pineapple shells to serve.

6 to 8 servings

Apple Sorbet

- 1½ lb apples, peeled and sliced
- 2 cups water
- Grated rind and juice of 1 lemon
- ¾ cup sugar
- 1 egg white
- 1 to 2 tablespoons Calvados or applejack

Simmer the apples with ¾ cup of the water in a large covered saucepan over low heat until soft. Cool slightly.

Puree the apples, lemon rind and juice in a blender until smooth.

Gently heat the remaining water with the sugar, stirring until dissolved. Boil for 5 minutes; let cool. Stir in the apple puree. Pour into a freezer container; cover and freeze for 3 hours, until partially frozen.

Beat the egg white until stiff; fold into the partially frozen ice. Cover and freeze for 2 hours. Fold in the Calvados. Cover and freeze until firm.

Ten minutes before serving, transfer to the refrigerator to soften. Garnish with mint leaves if desired.

6 to 8 servings

Apricot Ice Cream

- ¾ lb dried apricots, soaked in water for 2 hours
- 2 tablespoons lemon juice
- 3 egg whites
- ¾ cup sugar
- 1¼ cups whipping cream, whipped

Place the apricots and soaking liquid in a saucepan, adding water if necessary to cover. Simmer gently, covered, for 20 minutes. Reserve ⅔ cup of the liquid; drain the fruit and let cool slightly. Puree the apricots with the reserved liquid and lemon juice in a blender. Cool completely.

Beat the egg whites until stiff. Beat in the sugar. Then fold in the cream and apricot puree. Pour the mixture into a freezer container; cover and freeze until firm.

Thirty minutes before serving, transfer the ice cream to the refrigerator to soften. Spoon into chilled dessert dishes.

6 to 8 servings

Mint Ice

2 cups water
½ cup sugar
Finely shredded rind and juice of 2 lemons
¼ cup mint leaves
Few drops green food coloring (optional)
1 egg white

Combine the water, sugar, lemon rind and juice in a medium saucepan and warm, stirring, until the sugar dissolves. Increase the heat, bring to a boil and simmer for 5 minutes. Add the mint leaves, cover and let cool. Strain and add the food coloring.

Pour into a freezer container; cover and freeze until partially frozen.

Beat the egg white until stiff; fold into the partially frozen mint ice. Cover and return to the freezer until firm.

Ten minutes before serving, transfer to the refrigerator to soften. Spoon into chilled dessert glasses and garnish with frosted mint leaves if desired.

6 servings

Raspberry Ice

1 pint raspberries
½ cup sugar
⅔ cup water
Juice of ½ lemon
1 egg white

Puree the raspberries in a blender. Strain to remove the seeds.

Combine the sugar and water in a small saucepan and heat gently, stirring until dissolved. Increase the heat, bring to a boil and simmer for 5 minutes; let cool. Blend the syrup with the raspberry puree and lemon juice. Pour into a freezer container, cover and freeze until partially frozen.

Beat the egg white until stiff; fold into the partially frozen raspberry ice. Freeze until firm.

Ten minutes before serving, transfer to the refrigerator to soften. Scoop into chilled dessert glasses.

4 servings

Orange Sorbet

2 cups water
½ cup sugar
Finely shredded rind and juice of 1 lemon
1 can (6 oz) frozen orange juice concentrate, thawed
1 egg white

Combine the water, sugar, lemon rind and juice in a medium saucepan and heat gently, stirring until dissolved. Increase the heat, bring to a boil and simmer for 5 minutes. Let cool.

Strain the syrup and stir in the orange juice concentrate. Pour into a freezer container; cover and freeze until partially frozen.

Beat the egg white until stiff; fold into the partially frozen ice. Return to the freezer until firm, stirring once or twice.

Ten minutes before serving, transfer to the refrigerator to soften. Spoon into chilled dessert glasses.

6 servings

Raspberry Fluff

- 1 pint raspberries or 2 packages (10 oz each) frozen raspberries, thawed
- 2 egg whites
- ½ cup sugar (if using fresh berries)
- 1½ cups whipping cream, whipped
- 1 tablespoon Cointreau

Puree the raspberries in a blender until smooth. Strain to remove the seeds. Pour into a freezer container; cover and freeze for 1 to 2 hours, until partially frozen.

Beat the egg whites until stiff. Beat in the sugar, a tablespoon at a time. (The mixture should be very stiff.) Fold the whipped cream gently into the egg whites.

Beat the raspberry puree with a fork, then carefully fold it into the cream mixture along with the Cointreau.

Spoon into chilled dessert glasses and serve immediately.

4 to 6 servings

Bombe Grand Marnier

- 2 cups whipping cream
- 1 tablespoon powdered sugar
- ¼ lb homemade or bakery meringues
- 2 tablespoons Grand Marnier

Whip the cream until soft peaks form. Add the powdered sugar and continue whipping until stiff. Break the meringues into pieces and fold into the whipped cream with the Grand Marnier. Spoon into a 5-cup metal bowl or mold. Cover with foil and freeze until firm.

Thirty minutes before serving, unmold on a serving plate. Garnish with additional whipped cream and shredded orange rind.

8 servings

Avocado Ice Cream

- 2 ripe avocados, peeled and pitted
- ¾ cup half-and-half
- 1 cup whipping cream, whipped
- ½ cup sugar
- Juice of ½ lemon
- ½ cup chopped toasted almonds
- Vanilla wafers

Puree the avocados and half-and-half in a blender until smooth. Strain to remove any lumps. Turn into a large bowl and fold in the whipped cream, sugar, lemon juice and almonds. Pour into a freezer container; cover and freeze until firm.

Twenty minutes before serving, transfer to the refrigerator to soften. Spoon into chilled dessert glasses. Serve with vanilla wafers if desired.

4 servings

PIES, TARTS & CHEESECAKES

Lattice Crust Peach Pie

BASIC PIE CRUST:
- 1¾ cups all-purpose flour
- ½ teaspoon salt
- ½ cup butter
- 3 to 4 tablespoons ice water

FILLING:
- 5 cups sliced peaches
- ¾ cup sugar
- 3 tablespoons flour
- ¼ teaspoon ground nutmeg
- ¼ teaspoon ground cinnamon
- Pinch of salt
- 2 tablespoons butter

To make the pastry, sift the flour and salt into a bowl. Cut in the butter until the mixture resembles coarse crumbs. Add the water, a tablespoon at a time, and mix to a firm dough. Form into a ball and knead lightly.

Roll out ⅔ of the dough into an 11-inch round. Use to line a 9-inch pie pan. Chill the shell and remaining dough for 15 minutes.

Toss the peaches in the sugar, flour, nutmeg, cinnamon and salt until well coated. Turn into the pie shell and dot with butter. Roll out the remaining dough and cut into long narrow strips. Twist and arrange in a lattice pattern over the pie. Flute the edge.

Bake in a 400° oven for 25 to 30 minutes, or until the filling is set. Serve warm, with cream.

8 to 10 servings

Lemon Meringue Pie

- 1 recipe Basic Pie Crust (opposite)
- ½ cup cornstarch
- 1¼ cups water
- 2 tablespoons butter
- Grated rind and juice of 2 lemons
- 2 eggs, separated
- ¾ cup sugar

Roll the dough out into a 10-inch round and use to line an 8-inch pie pan. Line the pastry with aluminum foil and fill with pie weights or dried beans. Bake in a 400° oven for 15 to 20 minutes. Remove the foil and beans and return the crust to the oven for 5 minutes. Cool.

Blend the cornstarch with a little of the water in a small saucepan. Add the remaining water and the butter. Bring to a boil slowly, stirring constantly. Reduce the heat and simmer, stirring, for 3 minutes. Remove from the heat; stir in the lemon rind and juice, egg yolks and ¼ cup of the sugar. Pour into the pie crust.

Beat the egg whites until very stiff. Beat in the remaining sugar. Spread over the lemon filling. Bake in a 400° oven for 8 to 10 minutes, or until lightly browned. Serve cold.

6 to 8 servings

Deep-Dish Apple Pie

- 1½ lb tart apples, peeled and thinly sliced
- ½ cup packed brown sugar
- 1 teaspoon ground cinnamon
- ½ teaspoon grated nutmeg
- ¼ teaspoon ground cloves
- ½ recipe Basic Pie Crust (page 58)
- Water and sugar to glaze

In a deep 9-inch pie pan, layer the apples with the sugar and spices, finishing with a layer of apples.

Roll the dough out into an 11-inch round. Cut off a narrow strip all around and press firmly in place around the rim of the pie pan. Brush with water.

Use the rolling pin to lift the dough round onto the pie pan. Press the edge down firmly, seal well, trim and flute. Make a vent in the center. Brush the crust top with water and sprinkle with sugar. Bake in a 400° oven for 30 to 40 minutes.

Serve warm or cold.

4 to 6 servings

Deep-Dish Apple-Blueberry Pie: Use 1 lb tart apples and 1 cup blueberries. Omit the cinnamon and ground cloves. Layer the blueberries with the apples and nutmeg and proceed as directed.

French Apple Tart

SWEET PIE CRUST:
- 1½ cups all-purpose flour
- 6 tablespoons butter, cut into pieces
- ⅓ cup sugar
- 3 egg yolks
- ⅛ teaspoon vanilla

FILLING:
- 3 lb tart apples, peeled and thinly sliced
- ¼ cup sugar
- ¼ cup apricot jam
- Juice of ½ lemon

Sift the flour onto a marble slab or cold work surface. Make a well in the center and add the butter, sugar, egg yolks and vanilla. Work the ingredients together with the fingers, drawing in the flour little by little. Form into a ball and knead until smooth; chill for 1 hour.

Roll out the dough very thinly and use to line a 10-inch flan or quiche pan. Starting in the center of the pan, arrange the apples in an overlapping spiral pattern. Sprinkle with the sugar.

Bake in a 375° oven for 35 to 40 minutes, until the pastry is golden and the apples are tender.

Meanwhile, heat the jam with the lemon juice in a small saucepan. Strain and brush over the apples. Serve hot or cold, with whipped cream.

8 servings

Blueberry Lattice Pie

PASTRY:
- 1¾ cups all-purpose flour
- ½ teaspoon salt
- ½ cup butter
- 3 to 4 tablespoons ice water

FILLING:
- 1 pint blueberries
- ¼ cup water
- ½ cup packed brown sugar
- 1 tablespoon cornstarch
- ½ teaspoon ground cinnamon
- 2 teaspoons grated lemon rind
- 1 tablespoon lemon juice
- Granulated sugar

Sift the flour and salt into a bowl. Cut in the butter until the mixture resembles coarse crumbs. Add the water, a tablespoon at a time, and mix to a firm dough. Form into a ball and knead lightly.

Roll out ⅔ of the dough into an 11-inch round. Use to line a 9-inch pie pan. Chill the shell and remaining dough for 15 minutes.

For the filling, combine the blueberries, water and brown sugar in a saucepan. Cover and simmer for 10 minutes. Stir in the cornstarch, cinnamon, lemon rind and juice and simmer until the mixture thickens. Let cool. Spoon into the pie shell.

Roll out the remaining dough and cut into long narrow strips. Arrange them in a lattice pattern over the pie. Brush with water and sprinkle with the sugar.

Bake in a 400° oven for 25 to 30 minutes, until the crust is golden.

8 to 10 servings

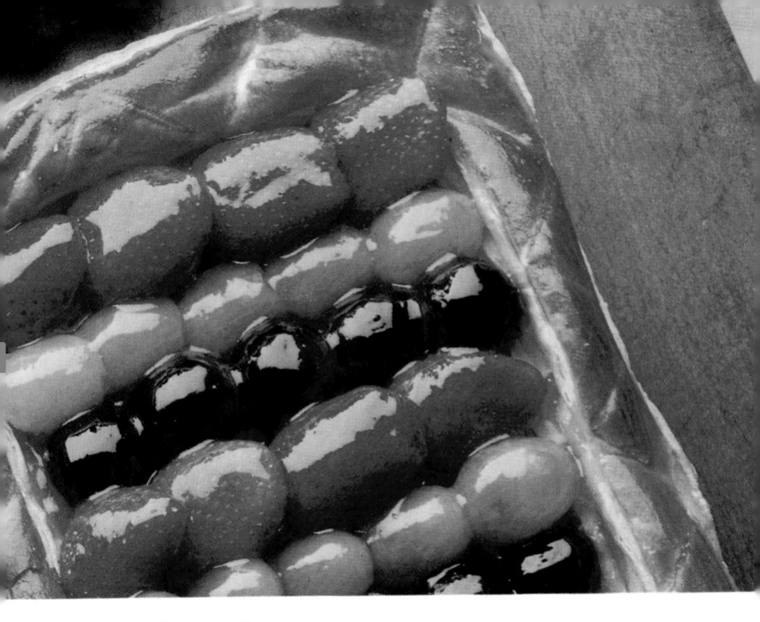

Glazed Fruit Tart

- 1 sheet (½ of a 17¼-oz package) frozen puff pastry, thawed
- Flour
- 1 egg yolk, mixed with 1 teaspoon water
- ¼ cup apricot jam
- 2 tablespoons water
- 1 teaspoon lemon juice
- ½ pint strawberries
- ¼ lb seedless green grapes
- ¼ lb black grapes, pitted

Roll the pastry out into a 12 × 8-inch rectangle. Sprinkle lightly with flour and fold in half lengthwise. Cut a 1½-inch-wide band from around the three open edges, leaving a 9 × 2½-inch folded rectangle. Open out the rectangle and roll out to 12 × 8 inches. Place on a dampened baking sheet, prick with a fork and dampen the edges. Open the band of pastry and position on the rectangle to make a border. Score a zigzag pattern on the border with a knife. Brush the border with the egg yolk mixture. Bake in a 425° oven for 20 to 25 minutes, until golden brown.

Warm the jam with the water and lemon juice in a small saucepan. Strain and reheat. Brush over the pastry base. Arrange the fruit on the pastry, alternating rows of strawberries, green grapes and black grapes. Brush generously with the remaining glaze. Chill.
6 servings

Raisin Cheesecake

6 tablespoons butter
½ cup granulated sugar
Grated rind and juice of 1 lemon
1½ cups cream-style cottage cheese
2 eggs, separated
½ cup ground almonds
¼ cup flour
½ cup golden raisins
Powdered sugar

Cream the butter, sugar and lemon rind together in a mixer bowl until light and fluffy. Beat in the cottage cheese gradually. Add the egg yolks and beat thoroughly. Stir in the almonds, flour, raisins and lemon juice.

Beat the egg whites until stiff; carefully fold into the cheese mixture.

Spoon into a greased 8-inch springform pan. Bake in a 350° oven for 50 to 60 minutes. Turn off the heat and leave the cheesecake in the oven until cooled.

Remove from the pan and sprinkle with the powdered sugar.

6 to 8 servings

Rich Chocolate Cheesecake

- ¼ cup butter, melted
- 2 cups graham cracker crumbs
- ⅓ cup packed brown sugar
- 6 oz semisweet chocolate
- 1 package (8 oz) cream cheese, softened
- ½ cup granulated sugar
- 2 eggs, separated
- ¾ cup whipping cream, whipped

Combine the melted butter, graham cracker crumbs and brown sugar. Press the mixture firmly onto the bottom and side of a 9-inch springform pan. Refrigerate until firmly set.

Melt the chocolate in the top of a double boiler over hot water. Beat the cream cheese, granulated sugar and egg yolks in a mixing bowl. Stir in the chocolate. Fold in half the whipped cream.

Beat the egg whites until stiff; fold into the cheese mixture. Pour into the crumb crust. Refrigerate until set.

Garnish with whipped cream and grated chocolate or tiny chocolate curls if desired.

6 servings

Note: Make chocolate curls by shaving thin layers from a block of chocolate with a vegetable peeler.

CAKES & COOKIES

One-Bowl Layer Cake

½ cup butter
½ cup sugar
2 eggs
1 cup all-purpose flour, sifted
2½ teaspoons baking powder
½ teaspoon salt

FROSTING:
½ cup butter
2 cups powdered sugar, sifted
3 tablespoons strong hot coffee
1 teaspoon vanilla

Warm the mixer bowl and beaters. Place the cake ingredients in the bowl and beat on low speed until combined. Increase to highest speed and beat for 40 seconds.

Divide the batter between two greased and lightly floured 7-inch round layer pans. Bake in a 325° oven for 30 to 35 minutes, until the cakes spring back when pressed lightly. Turn onto a rack to cool.

To make the frosting, combine the butter, powdered sugar and coffee in a mixer bowl and beat on low speed until combined. Beat on high speed until light and fluffy. Beat in the vanilla.

Spread the frosting over one layer; top with the second layer and frost the side and top of the cake.

Makes one 7-inch layer cake

Quick Sponge Cake

4 eggs
⅔ cup sugar
1 cup flour
FILLING:
1 quart strawberries, sliced
½ cup sugar
1 cup whipping cream, whipped

Combine the eggs and sugar in a mixer bowl and beat on high speed for 5 to 7 minutes, until very thick.

Carefully fold in the flour with a metal spoon. Divide the batter between two greased and lightly floured 8-inch layer pans. Bake in a 375° oven for 30 to 35 minutes, until the cakes spring back when pressed lightly. Turn onto a rack to cool.

Combine the strawberries and sugar; let stand 1 hour. Spread half the cream on one layer; add half the strawberries. Top with the remaining layer, whipped cream and strawberries.

Makes one 8-inch layer cake

Chocolate Chip Cake

- ¾ cup butter
- ¾ cup sugar
- 3 eggs
- 2 cups all-purpose flour
- 2 teaspoons salt
- 1 tablespoon baking powder
- 1 cup semisweet chocolate chips
- ½ cup ground almonds
- 2 tablespoons milk
- ¼ cup chopped almonds

Beat the butter and sugar in a mixer bowl on medium speed until combined; increase speed to high and beat until light and fluffy. Add the eggs, one at a time, beating in 1 tablespoon of the flour with the last two.

Fold in the remaining flour, the salt, baking powder, chocolate chips and ground almonds with a metal spoon. Fold in the milk.

Pour the mixture into a greased and lightly floured 7-inch round layer pan and sprinkle with the chopped almonds. Bake in a 350° oven for 1½ hours.

Leave in the pan for 5 minutes, then turn onto a rack to cool.

Makes one 7-inch cake

Chocolate Layer Cake

1 cup all-purpose flour
2 teaspoons baking powder
Pinch of baking soda
½ cup unsweetened cocoa
¼ cup corn oil
1 cup sugar
2 eggs
½ cup milk
¼ cup whipping cream, whipped
2 oz unsweetened chocolate

Sift the flour, baking powder, soda and cocoa together into a mixing bowl. Add the oil, sugar, eggs and milk and beat with an electric beater on low speed until combined. Increase to medium speed and beat for 30 seconds.

Divide the batter between two greased and floured 8-inch layer pans. Bake in a 350° oven for 35 to 40 minutes, or until the cakes spring back when lightly pressed. Turn out onto racks and cool.

Spread all but 1 tablespoon of the whipped cream over the top of one layer and position the second layer on top of it. Warm the chocolate and remaining cream in the top of a double boiler over hot water until melted. Cool slightly, then pour over the cake and spread evenly.

Makes one 8-inch layer cake

Buttercream Frosting

- 6 tablespoons butter, softened
- 4¾ cups powdered sugar, sifted
- ¼ cup half-and-half
- 1½ teaspoons vanilla

Beat the butter with the sugar in a mixer bowl on low speed until combined. Increase speed to high and beat until fluffy. Beat in 2 tablespoons of the cream and the vanilla. Add additional cream to make spreading consistency.
Fills and frosts one 8- or 9-inch layer cake

Chocolate: Melt 2 oz unsweetened chocolate; add with the vanilla.
Mocha: Add ¼ cup cocoa and ½ teaspoon instant coffee with the vanilla.
Orange or Lemon: Cream 2 teaspoons grated orange rind or ½ teaspoon grated lemon rind with the butter. Substitute orange or lemon juice for the cream.

Cream Cheese Frosting

- 1 package (3 oz) cream cheese
- 1 tablespoon butter
- 1 teaspoon vanilla
- 2 cups powdered sugar, sifted
- ½ cup chopped pecans

Soften the cream cheese and butter. Combine with the vanilla in a small mixer bowl and beat on low speed until fluffy. Add the powdered sugar and continue beating. If necessary, add a little milk to make spreading consistency. Stir in the nuts.
Frosts one 8-inch layer cake

Creamy Chocolate Frosting

- 6 oz unsweetened chocolate
- 3 egg yolks
- 2¼ cups sugar
- ¾ cup milk
- 1½ tablespoons butter
- Pinch of salt
- 2 tablespoons vanilla

Melt the chocolate in the top of a double boiler over simmering water. Beat the egg yolks until thick. Add the sugar, milk and butter and simmer in a heavy saucepan over very low heat, stirring constantly. Do not let stick. Bring to a boil for 1 minute. Remove from the heat and stir in the melted chocolate, salt and vanilla. Beat until of desired spreading consistency.
Fills and frosts one 9-inch layer cake

Classic 7-Minute Frosting

- 1½ cups sugar
- ½ cup water
- 2 egg whites
- 1 tablespoon light corn syrup
- 1 teaspoon vanilla
- ½ teaspoon salt

Combine all the ingredients in the top of a double boiler. Beat with an electric mixer on high speed for about 1 minute.

Place over rapidly boiling water and continue to beat on high speed until soft peaks form, about 7 minutes. Pour the mixture into a mixer bowl and continue beating until thick enough to spread.

Fills and frosts one 9-inch layer cake

Chocolate Chip Cookies

½ cup butter
¼ cup sugar
1 egg, beaten
¾ cup all-purpose flour
1¼ teaspoons baking powder
¾ teaspoon salt
1 package (6 oz) semisweet chocolate chips

Beat the butter and sugar together until light and fluffy. Add the egg and beat thoroughly. Sift the flour with the baking powder and salt and fold into the creamed mixture with the chocolate chips.

Drop by teaspoonfuls, a few inches apart, onto a greased baking sheet. Bake in a 350° oven for 15 to 20 minutes. Cool on a rack.

25 to 30 cookies

Coconut Cookies

½ cup butter, softened
¾ cup sugar
1 egg, beaten
1¾ cups all-purpose flour, sifted
1¼ teaspoons baking powder
¾ teaspoon salt
¾ cup flaked coconut

Beat the butter and sugar together until light and fluffy. Add the egg and beat thoroughly. Stir in the flour, baking powder, salt and half of the coconut.

Shape the dough into walnut-size balls and roll in the remaining coconut. Place slightly apart on a greased baking sheet and flatten each with a spatula. Bake in a 350° oven for 10 to 15 minutes. Cool on a rack.

About 30 cookies

Cinnamon Crisps

1 cup whole wheat flour
½ cup rolled oats
⅓ cup sugar
½ teaspoon baking soda
1 teaspoon ground cinnamon
6 tablespoons butter
1 tablespoon dark corn syrup
1 tablespoon milk

Combine the flour, oats and sugar in a mixing bowl. Add the soda and cinnamon and mix thoroughly. Heat the butter, syrup and milk in a small saucepan until the butter melts. Pour into the dry ingredients and beat until smooth.

Shape into small balls. Place slightly apart on a greased baking sheet and flatten each with a spatula.

Bake in a 350° oven for 15 minutes, until golden brown. Cool on the baking sheet.

About 25 cookies

Refrigerator Cookies

½ cup butter
½ cup sugar
1 small egg, beaten
1 teaspoon vanilla
2 cups all-purpose flour, sifted

Combine the butter and sugar in a mixer bowl and beat until light and fluffy. Beat in the egg and vanilla. Stir in the flour and mix thoroughly.

Knead on a lightly floured surface until smooth. Shape into a long roll 1½ inches in diameter. Wrap in foil and chill for 1 hour.

Remove from the foil, cut into ¼-inch slices and arranges slightly apart on a baking sheet. Bake in a 400° oven for 7 to 8 minutes, until golden brown. Leave on the baking sheet for 1 minute, then transfer to a rack to cool.

About 50 cookies

Nutty Cookies: Stir in ½ cup chopped nuts with the flour.

Cherry Cookies: Stir in ½ cup chopped candied cherries and ¼ cup chopped angelica with the flour.

Chocolate Cookies: Replace 2 tablespoons of the flour with 2 tablespoons cocoa.

Chocolate Cookies

1½ cups all-purpose flour
1 teaspoon baking powder
Pinch of baking soda
6 tablespoons butter
¼ cup brown sugar
3 tablespoons dark corn syrup
½ cup semisweet chocolate chips

Sift the flour, baking powder and baking soda into a mixer bowl. Add the butter in pieces, and beat on low speed until the mixture resembles bread crumbs. Mix in the brown sugar and corn syrup; stir in the chocolate chips.

Form into balls about the size of walnuts; place slightly apart on a greased baking sheet. Press gently with a spatula to flatten slightly. Bake in a 375° oven for 15 minutes, until golden brown. Transfer to a rack to cool.

About 24 cookies

SPECIAL OCCASION DESSERTS

Gâteau Malakoff

- 6 tablespoons butter
- ½ cup sugar
- 1 egg yolk
- 1 cup ground almonds
- ½ cup half-and-half
- 3 tablespoons brandy
- 1¼ cups strong black coffee
- 24 ladyfingers, split
- ¾ cup whipping cream, whipped

Cream the butter and sugar together until light and fluffy. Beat in the egg yolk, ground almonds and half-and-half until smooth.

Combine the brandy and coffee; dip in the ladyfingers quickly. Arrange about a third of them on the bottom of a greased 8-inch springform pan. Spread with half the almond cream and top with another third of the ladyfingers. Cover with the remaining almond cream and arrange a layer of ladyfingers on top. Chill until set.

Unmold on a serving plate. Spread ⅔ of the whipped cream over the top of the cake; pipe the remaining cream around the edge. Garnish with slivered blanched almonds.

6 to 8 servings

Zucotto

- 1 recipe Sponge Cake (page 84)
- 1/4 cup brandy
- 2 cups whipping cream
- 1/4 cup powdered sugar
- 2 oz semisweet chocolate, chopped, or 1/2 cup chocolate chips
- 1/4 cup chopped toasted almonds
- 1/2 lb Bing cherries, pitted
- 2 tablespoons kirsch

Prepare the sponge cake batter as directed for Black Forest Gâteau (page 84). Pour into a greased 8-inch round layer pan. Bake in a 350° oven for 35 to 40 minutes. Turn out onto a rack to cool.

Slice the cake horizontally into two layers and use one to line a 1½-quart mold or bowl, shaping the cake to fit. Sprinkle with the brandy and set aside.

Whip the cream until soft peaks form. Fold in the powdered sugar, chocolate, almonds, cherries and kirsch. Spoon into the mold and cover with the remaining sponge cake. Cover with a plate to weight down and chill for 2 to 3 hours.

Invert the cake onto a serving plate and unmold. Decorate with powdered sugar and cocoa if desired.

6 to 8 servings

Crêpes Suzette

CREPE BATTER:
- 1 cup all-purpose flour
- ¼ teaspoon salt
- 1 egg, beaten
- 1½ cups milk
- 1 tablespoon oil

ORANGE SAUCE:
- ¼ cup butter
- ¼ cup sugar
- Grated rind and juice of 2 oranges
- 2 tablespoons Grand Marnier
- 2 tablespoons brandy

Sift the flour and salt into a bowl, making a well in the center. Add the egg. Gradually pour in half the milk, stirring constantly. Add the oil and beat thoroughly until smooth. Stir in the remaining milk and let the batter stand for 30 minutes.

Heat a 6-inch crepe pan until hot and add a few drops oil. Pour in 1 tablespoon of the batter, quickly tilting the pan to coat the bottom evenly. Cook over moderate heat until the underside is brown; turn and brown the other side 10 seconds. Repeat with the remaining batter, stacking the cooked crepes between squares of waxed paper.

To make the sauce, melt the butter in a 10-inch skillet. Add the sugar, orange rind and juice and heat until bubbling. Fold the crepes into quarters and place around the edge of the pan. Spoon the sauce over them. Add the Grand Marnier and brandy, warm and ignite. When the flames subside, spoon the crepes and sauce onto dessert plates. Serve immediately.

4 servings

Crêpes au Chocolat

CREPE BATTER:
1 cup all-purpose flour
¼ teaspoon salt
2 tablespoons sugar
1 tablespoon instant coffee
1 tablespoon cocoa
2 eggs, beaten
1¼ cups milk
1 tablespoon oil

CHOCOLATE SAUCE:
6 oz semisweet chocolate
⅔ cup water
1 teaspoon instant coffee
½ cup sugar

FILLING:
1½ cups whipping cream
¼ cup sugar
2 tablespoons rum

Sift the flour, salt, sugar, coffee and cocoa into a large mixing bowl; proceed according to instructions for preparing and cooking crepe batter in Crêpes Suzette recipe (opposite). Let cool.

To make the sauce, combine the chocolate, 2 tablespoons of the water and the coffee in a small saucepan. Heat gently until melted. Add the remaining water and the sugar; heat gently, stirring, until dissolved. Simmer, uncovered, for 10 minutes. Let cool.

Whip the cream until fairly stiff. Fold in the sugar and rum. Place a tablespoon of the cream on each crepe, roll up and place on a platter.

Just before serving, pour a little of the chocolate sauce over the crepes; serve the remaining sauce separately.

6 servings

Cherry Gâteau

- 3 eggs, separated
- ½ cup sugar
- Grated rind and juice of ½ lemon
- ½ cup all-purpose flour
- ¼ cup ground almonds
- 1½ cups whipping cream, whipped with ¼ cup sugar
- 1 can (21 oz) cherry pie filling
- ½ cup toasted chopped almonds

Beat the egg yolks with the sugar, lemon rind and juice until thick. Stir in the flour and ground almonds. Beat the egg whites until stiff and fold them into the mixture.

Pour into a greased and lightly floured 8-inch round layer pan. Bake in a 350° oven for 35 to 40 minutes. Turn out onto a rack to cool.

Slice the cake horizontally into two layers. Spread half the cream over one layer and top with the second layer. Arrange the cherries on top, leaving a 1½-inch border around edge.

Brush the cherry syrup around the side of the cake. Press the chopped almonds around the side. Pipe the remaining whipped cream onto the border on top.

6 servings

Strawberry Pastry Ring

- Choux Pastry (opposite)
- ¼ cup slivered almonds
- 2 tablespoons sugar
- 1 pint strawberries, sliced
- 1½ cups whipping cream, whipped
- Powdered sugar

Prepare the choux pastry as directed for Profiteroles (opposite). With a pastry bag or spoon, form a 1½-inch-wide ring of pastry, 8 inches in diameter, onto a dampened baking sheet. Sprinkle with the almonds and bake in a 425° oven for 15 minutes. Lower the heat to 375° and bake 20 to 25 minutes longer, until golden brown. Cool on a rack.

Fold the granulated sugar and half the strawberries into the whipped cream.

Split the ring horizontally. Spread the filling over the bottom half and cover with the remaining strawberries. Replace the top half. Sprinkle with powdered sugar.

6 servings

Profiteroles

Chocolate Sauce (page 79)

CHOUX PASTRY:

- ¼ cup butter
- ½ cup water
- ½ cup all-purpose flour, sifted
- 2 eggs, beaten

FILLING:

- 2 tablespoons powdered sugar
- ⅛ teaspoon vanilla
- 1 cup whipping cream, whipped

First make the pastry. Bring the butter and water to a boil in a saucepan. Reduce the heat and add the flour all at once, beating until the mixture comes away from the side of the pan. Remove from heat. Add the eggs a little at a time, beating vigorously.

Spoon or pipe small mounds of pastry onto a dampened baking sheet (about 1 tablespoon dough for each). Bake in a 425° oven for 10 minutes; then lower the heat to 375° and bake 20 to 25 minutes longer, until golden. Make a slit through each puff. Cool on a rack.

Make the chocolate sauce as directed in recipe for Crêpes au Chocolat (page 79).

To make the filling, fold the sugar and vanilla into the whipped cream. Pipe or spoon a little into the center of each puff. Arrange the puffs on a platter and drizzle with the sauce. Serve the remaining sauce separately.

4 to 6 servings

Chestnut Dacquoise

- 5 egg whites
- 1¼ cups sugar
- 1½ cups whipping cream, whipped
- 1 can (8 oz) sweetened chestnut puree
- 2 tablespoons brandy

Beat the egg whites until stiff. Then beat in 3 tablespoons of the sugar. Carefully fold in the remaining sugar.

Using a pastry bag fitted with a ½-inch plain tip, pipe three rounds of meringue, each 8 inches in diameter, onto a lightly greased baking sheet. Bake in a 200° oven for 1½ to 2 hours. Lift from the pans and cool on a rack.

Combine ¾ of the whipped cream with the chestnut puree and brandy. Spread half the filling over one meringue. Top with a second meringue and spread with the remaining filling. Cover with the third meringue. Pipe the remaining whipped cream around the edge. Sprinkle with powdered sugar and grated chocolate if desired.

8 servings

Strawberry Meringues

- 4 egg whites
- 1/8 teaspoon vanilla
- 2 1/4 cups powdered sugar
- 3/4 cup whipping cream, whipped
- 1/2 pint strawberries
- 2 tablespoons currant jelly, warmed

Beat the egg whites until stiff. Beat in the vanilla and powdered sugar, a little at a time, and continue beating until the meringue is very stiff.

Line a baking sheet with brown wrapping paper and draw eight 3-inch circles on the paper. Spread half the meringue over the circles to form bases. Spoon the remaining meringue into a pastry bag fitted with a large fluted tip and pipe around the inside edge of each base.

Bake in a 200° oven for 1 to 1 1/4 hours. Remove from the paper and cool on a rack.

Spoon a little whipped cream into each meringue shell and arrange the strawberries on top. Brush the warmed jelly over the berries to glaze.

8 servings

Black Forest Gâteau

SPONGE CAKE:
- 3 eggs
- ½ cup sugar
- ½ cup all-purpose flour
- 2 tablespoons cocoa
- 1 tablespoon oil

FILLING AND DECORATION:
- 1 can (16 oz) pitted dark sweet cherries
- 1 tablespoon arrowroot
- ¼ cup kirsch
- 1½ cups whipping cream, whipped with ¼ cup sugar
- Chocolate curls (page 65)

Beat the eggs and sugar in a mixer bowl until thick. Sift the flour with the cocoa and fold into the egg mixture along with the oil.

Pour into a greased 8-inch round layer pan. Bake in a 375° oven for 30 to 35 minutes, until the cake springs back when pressed lightly. Turn out onto a rack to cool.

Drain the cherries, reserving the juice. Blend a little of the juice with the arrowroot. Bring the remaining juice to a boil in a saucepan. Remove from the heat and stir in the arrowroot mixture; blend well. Return to the heat and simmer gently, stirring, until thick and clear. Add the cherries; let cool.

Slice the cake horizontally into two layers and sprinkle with the kirsch. Spread the cherry mixture in the center of one layer and pipe a border of cream all around it. Top with the second layer. Spread half the remaining whipped cream around the side of the cake and press the chocolate curls into it. Pipe the remaining cream on top.

6 servings

Crème Brûlée

4 egg yolks
6 tablespoons sugar
2½ cups whipping cream
¼ teaspoon vanilla

Beat the egg yolks with 2 tablespoons of the sugar. Warm the cream in the top of a double boiler over simmering water. Stir in the egg yolk mixture and cook, stirring constantly, until the mixture is thick enough to coat the back of a spoon. Add the vanilla.

Pour into six ovenproof ramekins. Place in a roasting pan filled with 1 inch of water. Bake in a 275° oven for 30 to 40 minutes. Remove from the pan and cool; chill overnight.

To finish, sprinkle the remaining sugar over the tops. Broil under a high heat until the sugar caramelizes. Cool; chill for at least 2 hours before serving.
6 servings

Strawberry Mille Feuille

- 1 sheet (½ of a 17¼-oz package) frozen puff pastry, thawed
- 1 pint strawberries
- ¼ cup powdered sugar
- 1½ cups whipping cream, whipped
- ¼ cup currant jelly
- 2 teaspoons water
- ¼ cup chopped toasted almonds

Cut the pastry sheet into three equal pieces and roll each out into a 5 × 12-inch rectangle. Place on baking sheets, prick with a fork all over and chill for 15 minutes. Bake in a 425° oven for 10 to 12 minutes, until golden brown; cool on a rack. Trim the pastry edges and reserve for decoration.

Coarsely chop half the strawberries. Cut the remainder in half and set aside. Fold the chopped strawberries and the sugar into the whipped cream.

Spread half the strawberry mixture over one strip of pastry. Place a second strip on top; spread with the remaining strawberry mixture. Top with the last strip.

Heat the jelly with the water. Brush over the top pastry layer to glaze and arrange the remaining strawberries on top. Brush with the remaining glaze. Crumble the reserved trimmings and combine with the almonds. Press onto the sides of the strip. Cut into 2-inch slices to serve.

8 servings

Crumb-Topped Cheesecake

- 6 tablespoons butter
- 2½ cups graham cracker crumbs
- ⅓ cup packed brown sugar
- 1½ cups cream-style cottage cheese
- ¼ cup granulated sugar
- 3 eggs, separated
- Grated rind of 1 lemon
- 2 envelopes unflavored gelatin
- ¼ cup water
- 1½ cups whipping cream, whipped

Melt the butter in a medium saucepan. Stir in the crumbs and brown sugar. Press half the crumb mixture firmly onto the bottom of an 8-inch spring-form pan. Chill until firm.

Combine the cottage cheese, granulated sugar, egg yolks and lemon rind in a mixer bowl and beat well. Stir the gelatin into the water in a small metal bowl. Set in hot water until the gelatin dissolves. Stir into the cheese mixture.

Fold ⅔ of the whipped cream into the cheese mixture. Beat the egg whites until stiff and fold into the mixture. Spoon into the prepared pan and chill 10 minutes. Sprinkle the remaining crumb mixture over the top and chill 2 hours.

Remove the cheesecake from the pan and decorate with the remaining whipped cream.

8 servings

Strawberry Cheesecake

1¼ cups graham cracker crumbs
6 tablespoons sugar
¼ cup butter, melted
2 envelopes unflavored gelatin
3 tablespoons water
1½ cups cottage cheese
Grated rind and juice of 1 lemon
2 eggs, separated
1¼ cups half-and-half
1 quart strawberries

Combine the cracker crumbs, 2 tablespoons of the sugar and the melted butter; mix well. Press the crumb mixture firmly and evenly onto the bottom of an 8-inch springform pan. Chill until firm.

Stir the gelatin into the water in a small metal bowl. Set in hot water until the gelatin dissolves. Combine the cheese, lemon rind and juice, egg yolks, half-and-half, gelatin and the remaining 4 tablespoons sugar in the blender. Whirl until smooth. Transfer to a bowl.

Beat the egg whites until stiff and fold into the cheese mixture. Pour into the springform pan and refrigerate until chilled and set.

Remove the cheesecake from the pan and arrange the strawberries on top. Decorate with whipped cream if desired.

8 servings

Hazelnut Meringue

MERINGUE:
4 egg whites
1 cup sugar
Vanilla
1 teaspoon vinegar
1 cup ground hazelnuts

FILLING:
1 tablespoon sugar
1 cup whipping cream, whipped
1 pint raspberries

Beat the egg whites until stiff, then beat in the sugar, 1 tablespoon at a time. Carefully fold in a few drops of vanilla and the vinegar and nuts.

Divide the mixture between two greased and waxed-paper-lined 8-inch round layer pans. Spread evenly. Bake in a 350° oven for 40 to 45 minutes.

Loosen the meringue layers from the pans with a sharp knife and turn out onto a rack to cool.

Fold the sugar into the whipped cream; combine with the raspberries, reserving a little of each for decoration. Spread the filling over one layer; gently top with the other layer. Sprinkle with powdered sugar if desired. Decorate with the reserved whipped cream and raspberries.

6 servings

Walnut Dacquoise

MERINGUE:
4 egg whites
1 cup sugar
½ cup ground walnuts

FILLING:
½ cup sugar
¼ cup water
¼ cup hot black coffee
2 cups whipping cream, whipped

Beat the egg whites until stiff, then beat in 2 tablespoons of the sugar. Fold in remaining sugar and the nuts. Spoon or pipe the meringue into two 8-inch rounds on a baking sheet lined with brown wrapping paper. Bake in a 175° oven for 1½ to 2 hours. Transfer to a rack to cool.

To make the filling, gently heat the sugar and water in a saucepan until dissolved. Increase the heat and boil to a rich brown caramel. Remove from the heat and carefully add the coffee. Stir until caramel has melted, heating again if necessary. Let cool.

Fold the whipped cream into the caramel and spread ¾ of it over the top of one meringue. Place the second meringue on top. Garnish with rosettes of the remaining whipped cream and, if desired, walnut halves.

6 servings

Red Velvet Cake

1¼ cups sugar
½ cup butter
2 eggs
½ teaspoon salt
3 tablespoons cocoa
2 tablespoons water
1 teaspoon red food coloring
2½ cups cake flour
1½ teaspoons baking powder
1 cup buttermilk
1 teaspoon baking soda
1 tablespoon vinegar

Beat the sugar and butter in a mixer bowl until light and fluffy. Beat in the eggs, one at a time. Mix the salt, cocoa, water and food coloring; stir into the creamed mixture.

Sift the flour with the baking powder. Add half the flour to the creamed mixture and blend well. Blend in half of the buttermilk. Add the remaining flour and blend. Stir in the remaining buttermilk. Mix the soda and vinegar; gently fold into the batter.

Divide the batter between two greased and floured 9-inch round layer pans. Bake in a 350° oven for 25 to 30 minutes, or until the cakes spring back when pressed lightly. Let cool a few minutes before turning out onto a rack to cool. Fill and frost with Classic 7-Minute Frosting (page 71).

Apple Crepe Cake

Crepes (page 78)
2 tablespoons butter
1½ lb apples, peeled and sliced
⅓ cup packed brown sugar
¼ teaspoon each ground cloves and cinnamon
½ cup golden raisins
¼ cup apricot jam, warmed
¼ cup toasted sliced almonds

Prepare and cook the crepe batter as directed in the recipe for Crêpes Suzette (page 78).

To make the filling, melt the butter in a large saucepan. Add the apples, sugar, cloves, cinnamon and raisins. Cover and simmer over low heat for 10 to 15 minutes, until the apples are tender.

Lay a crepe flat in the center of a greased ovenproof plate. Spread some of the apple mixture over the crepe and top with another crepe. Continue layering the filling and crepes until all are used, finishing with a crepe.

Spoon the warmed apricot jam over the top of the crepe cake to glaze. Bake in a 350° oven for 10 to 15 minutes, or until heated through.

Sprinkle the sliced almonds over the top and cut into wedges to serve. Accompany with whipped cream if desired.

6 servings

Chocolate Mocha Roll

CAKE:
6 eggs, separated
Pinch of salt
½ teaspoon vanilla
⅓ cup granulated sugar
⅓ cup all-purpose flour
⅓ cup cocoa
Powdered sugar

FILLING:
1 tablespoon instant coffee
1 tablespoon boiling water
1½ cups whipping cream, whipped
2 tablespoons powdered sugar

In a mixer bowl, beat the egg whites with the salt until soft peaks form. Add the vanilla. Gradually add the sugar, beating until very stiff.

Break the egg yolks with a fork; pour on the meringue. Combine the flour and cocoa; sift over the mixture. Fold into the meringue with the yolks.

Spread the batter evenly in a greased 15½ × 10½ × 1-inch jelly-roll pan lined with greased waxed paper. Bake on the bottom rack of a 400° oven for 10 minutes, or until the top of the cake springs back when lightly touched.

Loosen the edges of the cake and turn out on a clean kitchen towel sprinkled heavily with powdered sugar. Cool on a rack. Peel off the waxed paper and trim the edges.

To make the filling, dissolve the coffee in the boiling water; let cool. Fold into the whipped cream along with the powdered sugar. Spread the mixture over the cake and roll up from the narrow end like a jelly roll. To serve, cut into 1-inch slices.

8 to 10 servings

INDEX

Apple(s)
bake, crisp, 31
baked stuffed, 35
Calvados, 36
crepe cake, 92
pie, deep-dish, 60
sorbet, 52
tart, French, 61
Apricot
ambrosia, 24
ice cream, 53
upside-down cake, 30
Avocado ice cream, 57

Banana(s)
flambé, 33
milk ice, 47
whip, 16
Black Forest gâteau, 84
Blackberry ice cream, 51
Blueberry lattice pie, 62
Bombe Grand Marnier, 56
Bombe Noël, 49
Bread and butter pudding, 29
Bread pudding, raisin, 26

Cakes
apple crepe, 92
apricot upside-down, 30
Black Forest gâteau, 84
chocolate chip, 68
chocolate layer, 69
chocolate mocha roll, 93
one-bowl layer, 66
quick sponge, 67
red velvet, 91
Charlotte
mocha, 11
Russe, 12
Cheesecake
crumb-topped, 87
raisin, 64
rich chocolate, 65
strawberry, 88
Cherry gâteau, 80
Chestnut dacquoise, 82
Chocolate
cheesecake, rich, 65
chestnut mold, 10
chip cake, 68
chip cookies, 72
cookies, 74
crêpes au chocolat, 79
layer cake, 69
mocha roll, 93
mousse, rich, 6
-orange mousse, 9
pots de chocolat, 22
Cinnamon crisps, 72
Coconut cookies, 72
Coffee and praline mousse, 10
Cookies, 72-74
Crème brûlée, 85
Crème caramel, 24
Crémets, 37
Crepe cake, apple, 92
Crêpes au chocolat, 79
Crêpes Suzette, 78

Dacquoise, 82, 90

Frostings, 70-71
Fruit
compote, red, 36
salad, molded, 39
salad, tropical, 32
salad, winter, 38
tart, glazed, 63

Gâteau Malakoff, 76
Grand Marnier, bombe, 56
Granita, pineapple, 52

Ice cream
apricot, 53
avocado, 57
blackberry, 51
chocolate, 46
coffee, 46
lemon-orange, 44
pineapple, 48
strawberry, 48
vanilla, 46
Ices, 47, 54
Indian pudding, 27